ALTERNATO
BOOKS

WORLD WAR II
ESCAPES AND
RESCUES

Matt Doeden

Lerner Publications ◆ Minneapolis

Lerner Publications Company
A division of Lerner Publishing Group, Inc.
241 First Avenue North
Minneapolis, MN 55401 USA

For reading levels and more information, look up this title at www.lernerbooks.com.

Main body text set in Aptifer Slab LT Pro Regular 11.5/18.
Typeface provided by Linotype AG.

Library of Congress Cataloging-in-Publication Data

The Cataloging-in-Publication Data for *World War II Escapes and Rescues* is on file at the Library of Congress.
ISBN 978-1-5415-2152-0 (lib. bdg.)
ISBN 978-1-5415-2156-8 (eb pdf)

Manufactured in the United States of America
1-44381-34646-12/18/2017

CONTENTS

INTRODUCTION
A DESPERATE RESCUE

Lieutenant Adrian Marks looked down on an endless stretch of blue on August 2, 1945. Marks and his crew had taken off in a seaplane from a nearby island to check on a report of wreckage in the ocean. As he arrived at the spot, Marks was horrified. The ocean was filled with men—US sailors.

Three days earlier, a Japanese submarine had attacked the USS *Indianapolis*. The *Indianapolis* started sinking quickly after that. Of the ship's crew of more than one thousand men, about three hundred went down with the ship. The rest abandoned the sinking vessel for the waters of the Pacific.

Marks's orders were to look and report only. But as he swooped his seaplane over the disaster scene, a shark attacked one of the sailors. Marks ignored his orders and landed his plane on the water.

The Japanese sub that sank the *Indianapolis* looms large in this photo from 1946.

Seaplanes such as this PBY Catalina played a role in nearly every major World War II operation.

Marks called for an emergency rescue as his crew began pulling men to safety. They managed to save fifty-six men, filling the plane and even laying sailors across its wings. They gave them what little water the airplane carried. And they waited.

The USS *Cecil Doyle* was the first ship to reply. It arrived at night. Its captain, W. Graham Claytor Jr., couldn't approach the sailors for fear of running them over in the dark. Instead of waiting idly until dawn, he turned on his ship's spotlight to help guide other ships to the site.

Over the next several days, more ships responded. They pulled 321 men from the water. The sailors were in rough shape. Yet all but four of the rescued sailors survived. Their tale of survival was just one of many dramatic rescues and escapes of World War II (1939–1945).

This crew of African American sailors earned the Navy Cross for demonstrating bravery after their narrow escape from an attack by the Japanese.

CHAPTER 1
BREAKING OUT

Battles during World War II were brutal. The **Axis** powers, led by Germany, Italy, and Japan, clashed with the **Allies**—the United States, Britain, the Soviet Union (a former country made up of fifteen modern nations), and others.

Soldiers captured by Axis forces faced terrible conditions in prisoner of war (POW) camps. The Japanese starved, beat, and forced the POWs to do hard labor. Many died. Almost all dreamed of escape or rescue.

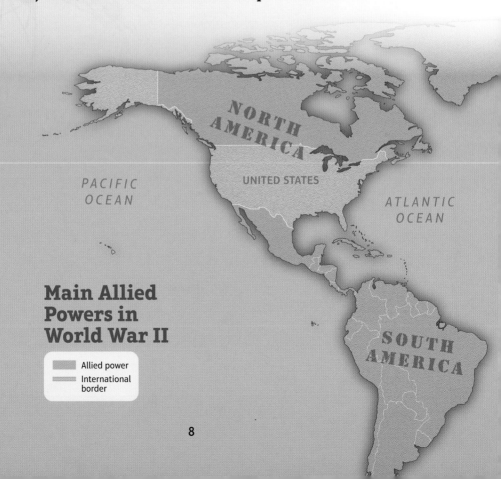

NORTH AMERICA

UNITED STATES

PACIFIC OCEAN

ATLANTIC OCEAN

SOUTH AMERICA

Main Allied Powers in World War II

- Allied power
- International border

TOM, DICK, AND HARRY

Stalag Luft III was a German POW camp south of Berlin, Germany. The camp held thousands of Allied POWs. It was one of Germany's most secure.

Yet British airman Roger Bushell planned to escape. Bushell organized a massive tunneling project. For close to a year, Allied prisoners chipped away, digging three tunnels. They named the tunnels Tom, Dick, and Harry. The Allies dug 30 feet (10 m) down to avoid microphones the Germans had placed underground.

BRITAIN

SOVIET UNION

ASIA

EUROPE

FRANCE

CHINA

AFRICA

PACIFIC OCEAN

INDIAN OCEAN

N

AUSTRALIA

The Harry tunnel was complete on March 24, 1944. Pilot Johnny Bull pushed through the ground, the first to make it outside the camp. Through the night, more prisoners followed. The trek through the tight tunnel was slow, and fewer than a dozen an hour could escape.

The Nazis quickly realized what had happened. They recaptured all but three of the escapees. The three men to make it out alive were pilots Per Bergsland, Jens Müller, and Bram van der Stok. Their survival was all thanks to Bushell's daring plan and the determination of the prisoners to carry it out.

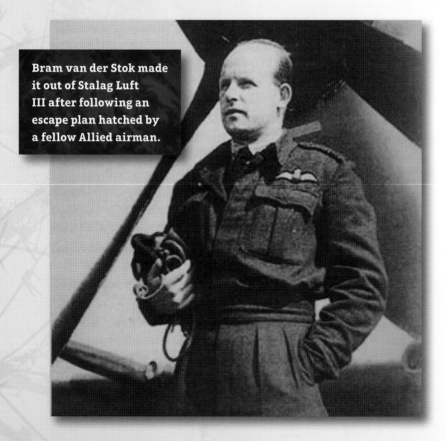

Bram van der Stok made it out of Stalag Luft III after following an escape plan hatched by a fellow Allied airman.

These men took part in the famous World War II mission that became known as the Great Raid.

THE GREAT RAID

Captain Robert W. Prince hugged the ground. Some 900 feet (274 m) of open land stretched between him and his goal: a Japanese POW camp outside the Philippines town of Cabanatuan. A team of about 120 men, mainly US Army Rangers, crawled across an open rice field. The land offered no cover.

The mission was urgent. It was 1945, and Japan had recently adopted a new policy. Guards were to leave no POWs alive to be rescued. Inside the camp, preparations for this kill-all order were under way. The clock was ticking.

A US P-61 Black Widow buzzed overhead. The pilot flew low to divert the attention of the guards and soldiers nearby.

The Rangers inched closer and then opened fire. The Japanese scrambled to respond. But they were unprepared. The fight lasted only about thirty-five minutes. About five hundred Japanese were killed. Only two Rangers died.

STEM HIGHLIGHT

The P-61 Black Widow was the first US warplane designed as a night fighter. The twin-engine plane came with built-in **radar**. The system detected objects even at night by bouncing radio waves off them and detecting the return signal. The P-61 could be used as a fighter or as a **reconnaissance** plane.

Some US Marines freed from the POW camp near Cabanatuan pose with the commander of the Rangers who rescued them.

Meanwhile, many of the POWs ran. Their time in captivity had left them fearful. Some thought the rescue attempt was a trick.

But they eventually realized the truth. The Rangers helped the half-starving prisoners out of the camp. They used shirts to make stretchers for the prisoners. The attack, later called the Great Raid, rescued all 512 prisoners in the camp.

CHAPTER 2
BEHIND ENEMY LINES

World War II soldiers, sailors, and airmen were at greatest risk when they were behind enemy lines. Units could be separated. Ships could be damaged and left behind. Some of the war's most dangerous missions were to rescue these men. Yet one rescue story stands out even among these heroic missions. The pilot at its center wouldn't give up no matter what. His determination and keen shooting skills helped save thousands. The mission was called Operation Dynamo.

German troops such as these posed a grave threat for Allied soldiers who found themselves behind enemy lines.

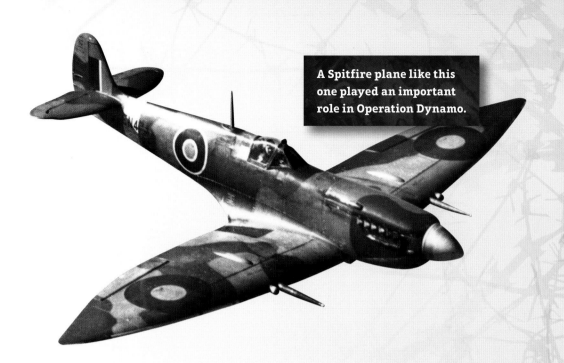

A Spitfire plane like this one played an important role in Operation Dynamo.

OPERATION DYNAMO

Royal Air Force (RAF) pilot Alan Deere looked down from his Spitfire fighter plane. Smoke hung over the beaches of Dunkirk, France, on May 28, 1940. Britain was staging one of the biggest rescue efforts of the young war. More than three hundred thousand British soldiers were stranded at Dunkirk. Desperate to rescue them, the British had enlisted a fleet of **civilian** ships and boats. More than seven hundred vessels answered the call. They weren't military ships. They were yachts, small motorboats, and fishing boats.

German planes swarmed the skies, dropping bombs on the fleet. The RAF put everything it had into shooting down the planes, trying to protect the boats. Deere was one of the RAF's best fighter pilots. He shot down German planes with incredible precision.

Deere attacked a German Do 17 fighter. But the German pilot was ready, firing his guns into Deere's Spitfire. Deere was going down. He tried to land on the beach. But the plane's nose slammed into the sand, knocking Deere unconscious.

HERO HIGHLIGHT

Virginia Hall was an American spy working for Britain during World War II. Hall posed as a US reporter in German-occupied France. Her real job was to train French resistance fighters.

Hall, known as the Limping Lady, had lost one leg in a hunting accident and used a wooden leg. When the United States entered the war in late 1941, Hall had to get out of harm's way. Physical challenges aside, she fled France on foot. She hiked over the Pyrenees mountain range and escaped into Spain.

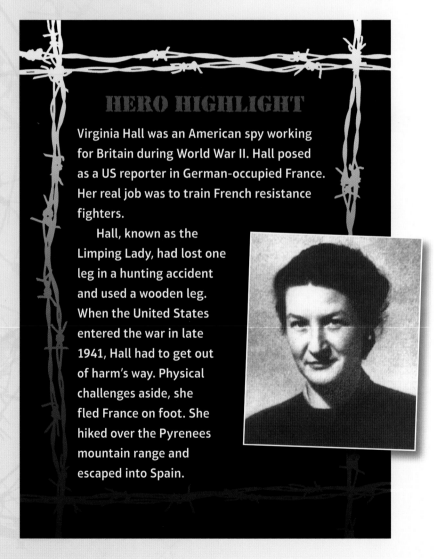

This little ship was one of many that responded to rescue Allied troops stranded at Dunkirk.

Despite suffering injuries from the crash, Deere came to and walked away. He hitched a ride on a boat across the English Channel. Just nineteen hours later, Deere returned to base. He didn't let the near-fatal crash deter him. He's credited with shooting down the most enemy aircraft of any pilot over Dunkirk.

The rescue effort was a huge success. Thanks in no small part to Deere staving off the enemy, the civilian fleet was able to rescue many thousands of British soldiers.

CHAPTER 3
LOST AT SEA

Airmen and sailors stranded at sea found themselves in grim situations. They often had no food or water. The sun beat down on them. Sharks circled. Most men lost at sea were never seen again. But a handful lived to tell their tales.

THIRTY-FOUR DAYS

Pilot Harold Dixon stood on the left wing of his Douglas Devastator bomber plane on January 16, 1942.

World War II fighter planes were tough, but they couldn't protect their pilots in the event of a crash at sea.

HERO HIGHLIGHT

Radio operator Morris Gillett stood on the deck of the destroyer USS *John W. Weeks* (*below*) on April 6, 1945. He watched as a Japanese attack destroyed a nearby US ship. The blast sent sailors flying into the water— and more sailors followed as they abandoned the sinking ship. The waters were dangerous, but Gillett didn't hesitate. He dove into the ocean and swam for the victims. He and fellow crew members pulled more than seventy men from the water.

It bobbed in the Pacific Ocean. Dixon and his crew, Gene Aldrich and Tony Pastula, were alive. But their situation was bleak. Their plane had run out of fuel. They struggled to inflate their emergency life raft as the plane slipped beneath the water's surface and disappeared. Suddenly the Japanese were not Dixon's greatest enemy. It was the sea.

Dixon and his men ended up on Puka Puka, one of the northern Cook Islands in the South Pacific, after their struggle to survive in the ocean.

The next day, Dixon and his crew began a thirty-four-day struggle. They collected rainwater. When sharks circled the boat, Aldrich speared one with a knife. They hauled it into the raft and ate it. But as time passed, the men grew increasingly hungry and **dehydrated**. By their thirty-fourth day, a storm was approaching, further threatening their survival.

On that day, Aldrich told Dixon that he saw a cornfield. Moments later, Dixon realized what it really was—an island. As it turned out, the people of that island, Puka Puka, were US allies in the war. They rescued the men and nursed them back to health. Against all odds, all three men survived.

THE ULTIMATE PRICE

US airmen Everett Almond and Art Reading were over the Pacific on May 16, 1943, when their plane's engine failed. Reading made a crash landing onto the ocean.

The force of the impact knocked Reading unconscious. The plane would sink quickly, so Almond had to make a choice. He could retrieve the plane's life raft, or he could save Reading. Almond chose to rescue his pilot. He attached a life vest to Reading and dragged him from the sinking plane.

Crashes into the sea were brutal and often fatal, even when they happened to seaworthy planes.

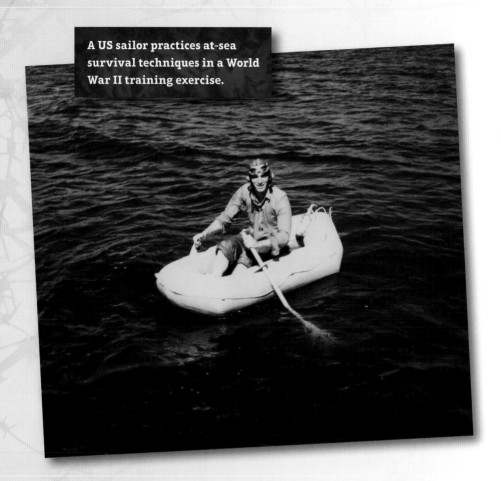

Reading slowly regained consciousness. Almond began swimming, towing Reading toward the nearest island, 20 miles (32 km) away. Soon, Almond noticed dark shapes in the water below: sharks.

One of the sharks bit down on Almond's leg. It pulled both men deep underwater. Then, suddenly, they popped back up to the surface. The shark had bitten off Almond's leg. Almond gave his life vest to Reading. Then he sank into the Pacific.

Reading remained in the water for eighteen hours, fending off constant shark attacks. He was beaten and battered but survived until a US ship could rescue him. Almond had given his life to rescue Reading.

STEM HIGHLIGHT

For airmen and sailors who found themselves in the waters of the Pacific, the Mae West life vest (*pictured below*)—named for a popular actress of the day—was the difference between life and death. The small rubber vests contained empty chambers. Each chamber was connected to a small cartridge of liquid carbon dioxide (CO_2). Anyone who fell into the water could simply pull a cord to unseal the cartridges. The liquid CO_2 instantly expanded and became a gas. It filled the chambers and made the vest a flotation device.

CHAPTER 4
MASTERS OF DISGUISE

World War II was filled with amazing escapes and rescues. Some relied on brute force or the element of surprise. Others took a little more creativity to pull off.

This image captures one of the war's many heroic rescues, showing one Allied ship aiding another after an attack.

FLOATING ISLAND

In February 1942, Japan's navy defeated the Allies in the Battle of the Java Sea. The surviving Allied ships fled. A few got left behind. That included the HNLMS *Abraham Crijnssen*, a Dutch minesweeper.

The ship was slow-moving, poorly armed, and all alone. It was a sitting duck for Japanese bombers. The crew was desperate. So they stopped at several small islands and cut down trees. The crew covered the ship with the trees. They hoped that Japanese pilots would mistake it for a small island.

It worked. Eight days later, the **camouflaged** ship reached Australia and safety.

It takes sharp eyes to spot the camouflaged *Crijnssen* in this photo.

Dutch resistance members such as Henk Drogt, shown here on a motorized bike, often used creative means to help Allied pilots.

EXPECTING?

US glider pilot George F. Brennan was on a mission over Holland when his glider was attacked. Bullet fragments slammed into his hand, leg, and face. Brennan managed to bring the glider to the ground, but he was captured.

Members of the Dutch resistance rescued Brennan. To hide him from the Germans, they disguised Brennan as a pregnant woman. They kept him in the maternity ward of a hospital until it was safe to return him to Allied forces.

A SIMPLE DISGUISE

The Germans called their prison at Colditz Castle escape-proof. But that didn't deter British officer Airey Neave. Neave hatched an escape plan so simple that the Germans never saw it coming.

Over months, Neave patched together a German uniform. Then, during a prisoner performance at the castle's theater, he and fellow officer Tony Luteyn dropped through a trapdoor in the stage. That led to a secret passage into the guard shack. From there, Neave and Luteyn simply strolled out through the courtyard. When a German guard challenged them, Neave appeared angry and demanded that the guard salute. It worked. The pair fled to Switzerland, escaping from right under the Nazis' noses.

Colditz Castle, near Leipzig, Germany

TIMELINE

September 1, 1939   World War II begins.

May 1940   Hundreds of thousands of British troops are stranded at Dunkirk in northern France. The British launch a rescue effort of more than seven hundred civilian craft.

January 5, 1942   British RAF officers Airey Neave and Tony Luteyn escape Colditz Castle.

January 16, 1942   Harold Dixon, Gene Aldrich, and Tony Pastula crash into the Pacific Ocean. They spend the next thirty-four days on a small life raft before landing on the shores of Puka Puka.

May 16, 1943   Everett Almond rescues Art Reading after their plane's engine fails. Almond dies after a shark bite, but Reading is rescued after eighteen hours in the water.

March 24, 1944   The Harry tunnel at Stalag Luft III is completed. A number of prisoners follow the tunnel outside the camp's walls, though all but three are soon recaptured.

January 1945	The Great Raid liberates more than five hundred POWs from a Japanese POW camp.
May 7, 1945	Germany formally surrenders, ending the European campaign of World War II.
July 30, 1945	A Japanese submarine sinks the USS *Indianapolis* into the Pacific, killing hundreds and forcing many others to abandon ship.
August 2, 1945	Lieutenant Adrian Marks begins the rescue of the sailors of the sunken USS *Indianapolis*. He and his crew pull fifty-six men from the water.
August 14, 1945	Shortly after the atomic bombings of Hiroshima and Nagasaki, Japan announces that it will surrender. World War II ends.

GLOSSARY

Allies: the nations that fought against the Axis powers during World War II. The Allies included the United States, Britain, the Soviet Union, and other countries.

Axis: the nations that fought against the Allies during World War II. Germany, Italy, and Japan led the Axis.

camouflaged: disguised to blend into the surroundings

civilian: not part of the military

dehydrated: lacking water in the body

radar: technology that bounces radio waves off objects to detect them at a great distance or in the dark

reconnaissance: the gathering of information on an enemy's forces and positions

FURTHER INFORMATION

BBC: World War II
http://www.bbc.co.uk/schools/primaryhistory/world_war2/

Benoit, Peter. *The U.S. Navy in World War II*. New York: Children's Press, 2015.

Ducksters: World War II
http://www.ducksters.com/history/world_war_ii/

Kallen, Stuart A. *World War II Spies and Secret Agents*. Minneapolis: Lerner Publications, 2018.

National Geographic Kids: "10 Eye-Opening Facts about World War 2"
http://www.ngkids.co.uk/history/world-war-two

Otfinoski, Steven. *World War II*. New York: Scholastic, 2017.

Owens, Lisa L. *Heroes of Dunkirk*. Minneapolis: Lerner Publications, 2019.

Index

Photo Acknowledgments

The images in this book are used with the permission of: iStockphoto. com/akinshin, (barbed wire backgrounds throughout); iStockphoto.com/ ElementalImaging, p. 1 (camouflage background); PhotoQuest/Getty Images, pp. 4–5; National Museum of the US Navy/flickr.com (CC 1.0 PDM), p. 6; National Archives (80-G-334029), pp. 7, 29 (left); © Laura Westlund/ Independent Picture Service, pp. 8–9; Wikimedia Commons (CC 1.0 PDM), p. 10; Bettmann/Getty Images, p. 11; Hulton Archive/Getty Images, p. 12; USMC Archives, from the John M. Cook Collection (COLL/1770) (CC BY 2.0), p. 13; National Archives (200-SFF-52), p. 14; NACA/Wikimedia Commons (CC 1.0 PDM), p. 15; iStockphoto.com/aaron007, pp. 16, 19 (barbed wire frame); Apic/RETIRED/Getty Images, p. 16; Stavros1/Wikimedia Commons (CC BY 3.0), p. 17; National Archives (80-G-65163), pp. 18, 29 (right); US Navy Photograph, from the collections of the Naval History and Heritage Command, pp. 19, 28; EwanSmith/Wikimedia Commons (CC BY-SA 3.0), p. 20; National Archives (80-G-K-15960), p. 21; National Archives (80-G-K-13770), p. 22; National Archives (80-G-K-13851), p. 23; National Archives (080-G-273880), p. 24; Australian War Memorial, p. 25; Yad Vashem via Getty Images, p. 26; SKOMP46866/Wikimedia Commons (CC BY 3.0), p. 27.

Cover: National Archives (080-G-281662-6) (lifeboat); iStockphoto.com/ akinshin (barbed wire background); iStockphoto.com/ElementalImaging (camouflage background); iStockphoto.com/MillefloreImages (flag background).